Jim
Rua

The Café Capriccio
Picture Book

The Café Capriccio Picture Book

Fantastic Food from the Chef's Table

JIM RUA

More Cookbooks from Café Capriccio

Café Capriccio, A Culinary Memoir (1990)

The Pasta Lovers Fast Food Cookbook (2000)

Café Capriccio's Chef's Table (2012)

Front cover image: Franco's prosciutto, aged two years

Cover and book design by Jessika Hazelton
The Troy Book Makers • Troy, New York • thetroybookmakers.com
Printed in the United States of America

To order additional copies of this title,
contact your favorite local bookstore
or visit www.tbmbooks.com

ISBN: 978-1-61468-245-5

Dedication

For the past couple of years I have been snapping smart-phone photos of the food Andrew Plummer and I prepare in the Chef's Table. This book is dedicated to Andrew who is a constant source of inspiration and a joyful collaborator. Thirty years of cooking with you, Andrew, is not enough, goddammit.

Introduction

This is the fourth book in a series that began almost 25 years ago with the publication of **Café Capriccio, A Culinary Memoir** (Capriccio Press, 1990). My intent is to chronicle the birth, life, and vicissitudes of Café Capriccio, a small Italian restaurant in Albany, NY, which I opened in 1982.

As with all lives and all business ventures whose fortunate fate is to endure for decades, the challenges, joys, sorrows, achievements, failures, and casts of attendant characters provide ample material for a documentary that may be interesting to persons other than the participants themselves. I hope it proves to be so with this quartet of Café Capriccio chronicles.

Unlike its predecessors, which were narrative tales, this is a picture book. I was tempted to eliminate narrative altogether, including recipes, but was persuaded that readers would appreciate brief descriptions of how these festive dishes are created. The approach I use here is to write succinct recipes for exactly what is shown in the photographs. For example, the recipe for spaghetti puttanesca is a recipe for the pictured dish, a bowl of pasta prepared for one person. These days, with recipes for all the world's favorite dishes instantly accessible on everyone's cell phone, home cooks need never be at a loss for recipe guidance. The principal objective of this book is to record what these dishes look like when served at Café Capriccio's Chef's Table, without disregard for basic recipes.

I do wish to emphasize for the reader (viewer) a few essential points:

- Each of these dishes was prepared as part of a meal served at the Chef's Table. Nothing in this book was created for the camera or for publication.

- All photos were taken with an iPhone camera—no special lighting, no props.

- The idea for this book struck me when I noticed on my cell phone more than one hundred photos of dishes from recent Chef's Table dinners that appeared to me exceptional.

- In ancient times—a few years ago—this book could not have been created because there was no way to take photos like these under "working" conditions.

- In all of my books and written recipes—and now photographs—I wish to emphasize the goodness of natural foods minimally processed, the virtues of simple preparation techniques, and the glory of imaginative presentations. Andrew Plummer's career exemplifies these values. His work and influences permeate this book, and Café Capriccio's cooking in general with which he has been associated for almost three decades.

- Along with Andrew, I also wish to acknowledge the late Chef George Reece, one of our most important mentors, whose influence on our cooking cannot be overstated.

- To Byron Nilsson I again express extreme gratitude for brilliant editorial contributions. Without your fine tuning, my friend, this book would look something like a Rorschack inblot test, I'm afraid.

Jim Rua

Spring, 2014

Porcini Mushrooms from the
San Lorenzo Mercato Centrale, Firenze

Roasted Plum Tomatoes
with Chinese Broccoli and Goat Cheese

10 ripe plum tomatoes cut in half lengthwise, 1½ pounds Chinese broccoli (available in Asian markets), 6 oz. crumbled goat cheese. Dried oregano, salt & pepper, olive oil.

Season the tomatoes with oregano, salt, and pepper. Drizzle with olive oil and bake at 300 degrees for about 1 hour. Steam the broccoli until tender. Let it cool. When the tomatoes are done, let them cool. Arrange the 3 ingredients as shown and finish with a fruity olive oil.

Grilled Sweet Mini Peppers with Eggplant and Arugula

2 eggplant sliced ¼ inch thick, 24 sweet mini peppers, 3 beaten eggs, flour for dredging eggplant, olive oil, 1 cup arugula roughly chopped.

Dredge eggplant in flour, coat with beaten eggs, fry in olive oil until golden on each side. Drain the eggplant on paper towels. Remove stems and seeds from the peppers. Grill the peppers over high heat until tender, about 4-5 minutes. Arrange the eggplant and peppers as shown and garnish with arugula. Serve at room temperature.

Calamari and Mussels Salad

2 lbs calamari tubes and tentacles, one dozen green shell mussels (these are sold on the half-shell), 1 cup cherry tomatoes cut in half, 1 cup olives, 2 tbl capers, 2 tbl chopped hot cherry peppers, flat parsley, basil, olive oil, juice from 3 lemons.

Poach the calamari in lightly salted water for 5 minutes. Keep covered and let stand for one hour. Cut calamari tubes into rings; cut up the tentacles or leave whole, your preference. Combine all ingredients; be sure the oil-lemon dressing is adequately distributed.

Arrange as shown or according to your own inspiration.

Encrusted Tuna with Shredded Cabbage

1 tuna loin about 6 inches in circumference, 6 inches long; 1 head of cabbage shredded, juice of 4 limes, olive oil, 4 tbl black peppercorns, 4 tbl coriander seeds, 4 tbl fennel seeds.

Toss the shredded cabbage with olive oil, lime juice, and a pinch of salt. Grind the spices together. Coat the tuna with the spices. Fry the encrusted tuna in olive oil on all sides. Turn frequently. Total frying time should not exceed 5 minutes. Allow the tuna to cool, then cut it as shown. Arrange the tuna over the shredded cabbage on a platter.

Greens with Roasted Peppers, Lime and Lemon

2 lbs of mixed greens like collards, kale, mustard, turnips. Two sweet red peppers. Juice from 2 lemons and 2 limes, several lemons and limes cut into wedges. Olive oil, salt & pepper.

Steam the greens until tender, about 5 minutes. Prepare the peppers by charring the skins over a gas flame or over charcoal. Let cool. Toss the greens with olive oil, lemon-lime juice, salt and pepper. Peel the blackened skin off the charred peppers, then slice the peppers.

Drizzle olive oil on the peppers; arrange with the greens, lemon, and lime wedges.

From Claudia and Iggy, Crisan Bakery, Albany, NY

Mixed Grill
Artichokes, Zucchini, Peppers, and Onions

Artichokes with stems packed in oil (available in Italian import stores), 2 large sweet red peppers, 3 small zucchini, 1 red onion, salt & pepper, oil from the artichokes.

Grill each vegetable separately, then combine them on a platter. Cut the artichokes in half, grill for one minute on each side. Slice the zucchini lengthwise ¼ inch thick, toss in artichoke oil, grill for a couple of minutes; core and seed the peppers, toss in oil and grill until tender; slice the onion and grill that. Assemble the dish on a platter. Serve at room temperature.

Ancient Communal Oven
at Fattoria Lavacchio,
Our Vineyard Home in Tuscany.

Join us there some time. Bring someone you love.

www.fattorialavacchio.com

Salad of Green Beans, Purple & White Potatoes, Corn, Tomatoes, and Olives

1 pound green beans with stems removed, 8 small potatoes cut in half (4 purple, 4 white), sweet corn from two ears, ½ cup olives, salt & pepper, olive oil.

Blanch the green beans for two minutes, then plunge them into cold water. Steam or boil the potatoes until tender. Cut the tomatoes in half. With a knife, remove sweet corn kernels from their stalks (no need to cook them). When the beans and potatoes are cool and dry, toss all ingredients together, season to your taste, and finish with olive oil.

Broccoli Raab with Sausage and Peppers

1 package of broccoli raab washed and cut up as shown, 2 dozen sweet mini peppers, 6 links Italian Sausage cut bite-sized. Olive oil, 5 cloves chopped garlic, salt & pepper.

Steam the broccoli raab until tender, about 2 minutes. Remove the core and seeds from the peppers. Sauté the sausage in a skillet with olive oil for 3 minutes, then add the peppers. Continue cooking until sausage is done, not more than 5 minutes further cooking. When the sausage is done, add the broccoli and garlic, stir and continue cooking for a couple of minutes. Arrange on a platter and serve.

Octopus with Pequillo Peppers, Olives, Zucchini, and Tomatoes

1 octopus weighing about 3 pounds. 1 small jar of Spanish Pequillo peppers (these are small wedged-shaped pimentos ubiquitous in Spanish cuisine). 2 small zucchini cut bite-sized, 2 ripe tomatoes cut into small pieces. 1 cup olives, 2 tbl capers, juice from 3 lemons, olive oil, parsley.

Poach the octopus in water slowly for 2½ hours. Allow the octopus to stand in the pot, covered, for another hour. Remove the octopus from the water and let it cool for 20 minutes. At this point it can be cut up for the salad. Add all other ingredients, leaving the Pequillo whole.

Toss well and arrange on a platter. Can be served chilled or at room temperature.

Asparagus with Grilled Tangerines

2 pounds of asparagus, bottoms trimmed. Several tangerines peeled, segmented as shown. Olive oil, salt & pepper.

Steam the asparagus for 1½ minutes, then plunge it into cold water. Remove after cooling and allow the asparagus to air dry. Drizzle the tangerines with olive oil, then grill over wood or charcoal, turning frequently. Grilling should take 2 minutes.

When the tangerines are cool, combine with the asparagus.

Long Hot Peppers with Garlic and Tomatoes

2 dozen long hot peppers, tops and seeds removed, otherwise left whole. 3 ripe tomatoes cut into wedges. Slivered garlic according to your taste for garlic. Olive oil, salt & pepper.

Wash the peppers. Drizzle with olive oil. Grill them over wood or charcoal for about 4 minutes, turning as necessary to ensure even cooking. Cool the peppers. Arrange on a platter with garlic and tomatoes. Season with salt and pepper, finish with olive oil. Best at room temperature.

Christmas Eve Spaghetti with Seven Fish(es)

6 littleneck clams scrubbed, 12 mussels, 1 pound calamari, 12 shrimp, 6 ounces fresh cod, 6 oz scallops, 6 oz scungilli (conch), 5 anchovies, 2 tbl capers, ½ cup chopped olives, one 28 oz can Italian plum tomatoes crushed by your hand, hot pepper to taste, 8 cloves chopped garlic, 2 tbl dried oregano, salt & pepper, olive oil.

Boil one pound of spaghetti in salted water for about ten minutes. Meanwhile, sauté garlic in olive oil for a minute, add tomatoes, anchovies, capers, olives, herbs, spices. Add the clams, cover and cook for 3 minutes, then add the rest of the fish.

Cook for 5 more minutes. Toss the pasta in this goodness; Buona Vigilia di Natale.

Italian Sausage, Onions, and Peppers al Forno

8 sausage links cut in half, 24 sweet mini peppers stems and seeds removed, 6 cipollini chopped (small white onions), 10 whole garlic cloves, olive oil, salt & pepper.

Arrange the ingredients in a skillet as shown on the previous page. Drizzle olive oil and season with salt and pepper. Bake for ½ hour at 375 degrees.

Going into the Oven

This is a photo of uncooked sausage, peppers and onions set in a skillet prior to baking in the oven. Baking, rather than frying such a dish, is fast and easy on the cook. On the next page is a picture of the result

Coming out of the Oven

Presented at the Table

In this photo I have taken the preparation from the skillet and arranged it in a beautiful serving bowl.

Grilled Peppers

Select several green and red peppers, remove stems and seeds.
Olive oil, salt & pepper.

Cut the peppers into strips, season with salt and pepper, toss in a small amount of olive oil then grill over high heat. Turn frequently. In this preparation, the peppers are blistered, as shown. Serve hot or at room temperature.

Roasted Plum Tomatoes, Grilled Radicchio, and Garlic Scapes

6 plum tomatoes cut in half lengthwise, seasoned with salt and dried oregano. 2 heads radicchio cut into quarters, 12 garlic scapes, ends clipped; olive oil.

Roast the tomatoes at 300 degree for 1 hour. Moisten the radicchio with olive oil.

Grill just enough to wilt the leaves, about 2 minutes per side. Steam the garlic scapes until tender, about 3 minutes. Combine all ingredients, adjust seasoning, arrange on a platter.

This is Fattoria Lavacchio's chef Sergio Giovannoni preparing our dinner on a recent visit: Bistecca Fiorentina

Paella Valenciana With a Mixed Salad.

Paella recipe can be found on our web site
www.cafecapriccio.com

Belgian Endive with Smoked Oysters, Mascarpone Cheese, Arugula

1 Belgian endive, 1 jar smoked oysters, mascarpone (a mild, soft Sicilian cheese), baby arugula.

Carefully remove the layers which constitute the Belgian endive. Arrange on each layer a dollop of mascarpone, one arugula leaf, and a smoked oyster. Crown with something red; here is pictured the top and stem from a small pepper.

Spaghetti with Clams Red

1 dozen littleneck clams scrubbed, 2 cups San Marzano tomatoes, 5 cloves garlic chopped, pinch of hot pepper, 2 tbl basil, 2 tbl parsley chopped, ¼ pound of spaghetti.

Boil spaghetti in salted water for about 10 minutes. Sauté garlic in olive oil for a couple of minutes, then add tomatoes and seasonings. Add the clams, cover and cook until the clams open. When the spaghetti is done, toss it in the sauce with clams and serve it in an appropriately festive bowl. Garnish with parsley.

*Antipasto : Franco's Cured Meats
with Cheese, Roasted Peppers, Olives, Arugula*

The meats are: prosciutto, sopressata, salami Calabrese, and capocollo. The cheeses are Crotonese and Gorgonzola. Calamata & Gaeta olives, roasted peppers, and arugula complete the dish.

Roasted Duck Leg with Pheasant Sausage, White Beans and Vegetables

1 duck leg and thigh, 2 links pheasant sausage (any sausage can be substituted), white beans (canned beans will work), green beans and red cabbage. Parsley, salt & pepper, olive oil.

Season the duck leg with salt and pepper and roast in the oven at 375 degrees for about 40 minutes until crisp and cooked throughout. Briefly fry the sausage in a skillet (4 minutes), add a can of beans, and cover and cook until the sausage is done, about 15 minutes. Blanch the green beans in salted water for 3 minutes then plunge into cold water. Chop the red cabbage and sauté in olive oil for a couple of minutes.

Add the green beans, mix well, then layer the vegetables, beans, duck and sausage on a plate. Garnish with parsley.

Salad of Arugula, Watermelon, and Shaved Asiago Cheese

3 cups of arugula, 10 scoops of watermelon using a melon baller, 1 oz of shaved Asiago cheese, salt & pepper, olive oil.

Season the arugula with salt and pepper, toss with olive oil, then arrange on a plate or in a bowl. Place the watermelon around the greens, add the shaved cheese and served chilled.

This is a photo of Fattoria Lavacchio, our vineyard home in Chianti, showing olive groves, two vineyards, Casa Bella — the main house where we often stay — the pool, and the patio where lunch is served on beautiful Tuscan days. The small brick building at left is the ancient forno di legna, the communal wood burning oven.

A vegetable market
in Firenze

Summer Supper: Grilled Steak with Peppers and Greens.

3 New York Strip Steaks each about 2 inches thick, 3 large peppers, 2 lbs greens, salt & pepper, olive oil.

Steam the greens then dress with olive oil, salt and pepper. Grill the steaks and the peppers. Slice the steaks and arrange with peppers over the greens.

Salad of Watermelon Radish, Pear, and Garden Vegetables

2 watermelon radishes cut in half then sliced, 2 pears cored and sliced, 1 cucumber peeled and cut up (seeds removed), the heart of 1 celery stalk, 1 small sweet red onion sliced, 5 or 6 radishes, sliced fennel, summer lettuce, chopped parsley, salt and pepper, olive oil, juice from 2 lemons.

Season to taste, drizzle olive oil, add lemon, toss and served chilled.

Arugula Pesto with Potato Gnocchi, Red Skinned Potatoes, Cream

2 cups arugula, 4 cloves garlic, 3 tbl salted nuts (pistachios are delicious), 1 oz grated Pecorino Romano, ¼ cup heavy cream, 2 oz olive oil, ½ cup red potatoes cut to about the size of potato gnocchi, 4 oz potato gnocchi.

Put all of the pesto ingredients into a blender and process until smooth. Boil the potatoes in salted water for 3 minutes. Add the gnocchi and cook for about 2 more minutes, until they rise to the top. Drain the gnocchi and potatoes, return them to the pot, and add the pesto and cream. Stir for a couple of minutes to integrate all ingredients. Serve hot in a bowl.

Vera Pizza Napolitana with Mushrooms,
Sausage, Shrimp, Mozzarella, Spinach, and Tomatoes

Clam Steam

2 dozen littleneck clams, scrubbed, 3 ears fresh corn cut into quarters as shown, ½ pound of butter, 2 tbl hot cherry peppers chopped, 3 shallots chopped, 1 cup dry white wine, pinch of black pepper, 4 ripe tomatoes cut into small wedges.

Combine all ingredients (except tomatoes) in a covered pot and cook until the clams open.

Add the fresh tomatoes, serve in a large bowl. See the following page for the result.

In the Pot, Ready to Cook
(at left)

Ready to Eat
(at right)

Steamed Asparagus with Grilled Mango and Grilled Oranges

1 pound asparagus cut in half, 3 oranges segmented, 2 mangoes cut into wedges, olive oil.

Steam the asparagus then plunge it into cold water. Toss the oranges and mango with olive oil, then grill over a hot flame for about 3 minutes. Turn frequently.

When the fruit cools, arrange it with the asparagus.

Spaghetti with Shrimp and Pomodorini (Grape or Cherry Tomatoes)

¼ pound spaghetti, 6 shrimp, 1 cup grape tomatoes cut in half, 5 cloves chopped garlic, juice from 2 lemons, pinch of hot pepper, chopped parsley, chopped basil, 3 tbl butter, olive oil.

Boil the pasta in salted water for about 10 minutes. Sauté the garlic in olive oil and butter for about a minute. Add the shrimp. Cook the shrimp for about three minutes, then add tomatoes, herbs and lemon juice. Toss around for another minute. Drain the pasta, toss it in the pan, finish with chopped parsley.

Zuppa di Pesce

6 littleneck clams scrubbed, 6 mussels cleaned, beards removed, 2 calamari tubes and tentacles cut up, 4 shrimp, 3 oz. scallops, 1 cup Italian peeled tomatoes, 5 cloves chopped garlic, 1 tbl capers, a few anchovies, chopped olives, pinch of hot pepper, chopped basil, chopped parsley, olive oil.

Sauté garlic in olive oil for a minute, add tomatoes and seasonings. Add clams, cover and cook for 4 minutes. Add all other ingredients and cook for about 4 minutes more, keeping the pan covered. Serve in a shallow bowl.

Chocolate Covered Strawberry Cheesecake
by Danielle Corellis,
Café Capriccio's Pastry Chef and Pizzaiola

White Clam Sauce
Taught to Me By My Esteemed Cousin, the Late, Great Michael Tiano

1 dozen littleneck clams scrubbed, 1 oz olive oil, 4 cloves chopped garlic, a few anchovies, chopped flat parsley.

Heat the oil, add the clams, cover and cook over medium heat until the clams begin to release liquid. Add garlic and anchovies. Cover again and cook for several minutes until all clams are open. Here is pictured white clam sauce with spaghetti. This sauce can be made during the 10 minutes it takes to cook the spaghetti.

This is my late, great cousin Michael Tiano who taught me many things, including how to make white clam sauce, described on the previous page.

Chanterelle in a Pan with Butter, Olive Oil, Garlic, Tomatoes, and Herbs

What would you do with this?

Franco Rua
and Jim Rua

Some of Franco's cured
meats in the hanging room

Franco's Sopressata
with Our Own Bread"

Franco Rua and Jim Rua
showing off their pizza in Saratoga Springs (*above*)

James L. Rua,
born to Franco and
Amanda on Jan. 6,
2008, inspecting
piglets (*at left*)

The Author, Winter, 2014

I jumped into the restaurant business on a dare almost 40 years ago: Hell, I can do that. My initial fling (the late and lamented Casa Verde) lasted almost 4 years and then I had enough. Six months later I was back at it with a memorable 3 year summer experience producing a supper club for patrons of the Tanglewood Music Festival in the Serge Koussevitsky estate named Seranak, located on the magnificent festival grounds. Then to Cafe Capriccio where we have been nestled for more than 30 years. No plans to retire and I expect Franco Rua to carry on for at least another generation. Despite the well documented hardships of restaurant ownership, I early-on felt that there was virtually nothing of interest to me that could not be integrated into the context of the restaurant life: family, cultural interests, culinary arts, travel, business, writing, friendships, socialization... And so it has been, clearly the right choice for one who looks forward to going to work every day. A blessing, really. I'm grateful and thank everyone who has been part of it. The 4 books tell a large part of the story, for anyone interested.